What is the Gospel? Straightforward Talks on Evangelism

with himself for time and eternity sinful, sinning, sin-saturated human beings. But that is inconceivable. A holy, sinless God *cannot* ignore sin.

Well, then, God might let all men for time and eternity receive the full, inevitable consequences of their sin, thereby being forever separated and cut off from fellowship with Him. Thus all human beings would go to hell, forever lost. This also is unthinkable; God did not create the human race in his own image to have that race, in its entirety, forever lost.

There is only one other possibility. God cannot ignore sin; and God cannot ignore man. Then God himself must pay the penalty of man's sin in order that man may be saved, while at the same time sin is taken fully into account and dealt with as the black, heinous fact that it is.

God *cannot* condone sin; he *must* condemn it. The wages of sin is death; and God cannot set aside or abrogate those wages while he continues to be a holy and righteous God. If only a single member of the human race is to be saved from paying the death penalty of sin, God must pay that penalty himself. And that is the necessity for the death of Christ. His death indeed showed forth the supreme love of God for men. But we see that it did infinitely more.

In our human way we may, as it were, think of the members of the Godhead, far back in the infinite reaches of eternity, before ever creation

Trumbull

What is the Gospel?

STRAIGHTFORWARD TALKS ON EVANGELISM

By
CHARLES GALLAUDET TRUMBULL
Editor of The Sunday School Times

THE SUNDAY SCHOOL TIMES CO.
PHILADELPHIA

Copyright, 1918, by
The Sunday School Times Company

Second Printing, December, 1918

The price of this book is 35 cents, in paper;
or 50 cents, in cloth binding; postpaid.

CONTENTS

————

Books and pamphlets recommended for further study are mentioned on pages 78, 79, and 80.

A FOREWORD

By the General Secretary of the Evangelistic Committee of New York City

HAVING learned that the laymen of Great Britain were unusually active in evangelistic endeavor, I crossed the Atlantic in 1909 to make a study of the work they were doing. To my surprise, I learned that there were less than 10,000 ordained preachers and over 50,000 unordained preachers in the non-conformist churches. I found an organization in London with about 400 members who were available for evangelistic work at the weekends, at their own charges. Some of these men were members of the House of Lords and the House of Commons. They were bankers, barristers, manufacturers, merchants, etc. I found another organization with about 750 members who were available for open-air meetings. There were similar organizations throughout England, Scotland, and Ireland.

During the voyage home I asked God to help me contribute a little at least toward encouraging lay workers in New York City to engage in aggressive evangelistic work. Realizing the truth of the old adage, "It is difficult to teach an old dog new tricks," I began with the point of least resistance, the Young People's Societies. We conducted Evangelistic Institutes in which the representatives of these societies were taught the evangelistic message and evangelistic methods, having on our platform some of the most eminent teachers in the East. Gradually members of men's organizations in the churches and representatives of the Y. M. C. A. participated in the institutes. As a result, during the season of 1917 over eleven hundred meetings were conducted by these volunteers, and the Gospel was preached to over 260,000 persons.

Mr. Charles Gallaudet Trumbull, Editor of The Sunday School Times, gave seven lectures on The Evangelistic Message at the Evangelistic Institute in 1918. Although the attendance at this institute was not as large as it has been in other years, which is easily accounted for by the absence of so many of the young men who are "with the colors," the interest was deeper than it has ever been. This was doubtless due to the fact that Mr. Trumbull, avoiding controversy, presented the Gospel message so clearly that the man in the street could understand it.

Interest in things vital is increasing. The spirit of lay evangelism is spreading throughout the world. Lay workers are assuming the responsibility that God gave in the great commission, "Go . . . and preach the gospel . . . " It is possible that more aggressive evangelistic work is being done for the soldiers in our army

On Evangelism

than has ever been done in the history of any army in any country in the world. Women are eager to do their "bit." In many instances they are filling the gaps in church work as well as in business left by the young men who have gone into the service. They have even gone so far as to take charge of open-air meetings that formerly were led by young men. Some of them are giving the message in public.

These lectures by Mr. Trumbull make the message so clear that it is easy for lay workers to grasp it. The undersigned earnestly hopes that the lectures will have a large circulation, that they may be used as a basis for study in institutes throughout the land. Such institutes do not always need a living teacher. Frequently a text-book such as this can be used effectively. Those who desire to "be fit for more than they are now doing" for Christ can take these lectures as a basis for group study, electing one of their own number as leader. Every Young People's Society in the land can increase its efficiency by mastering The Evangelistic Message as it is given here in "What is the Gospel?"

ARTHUR J. SMITH.

I

WHY MEN ARE LOST

Sin and Its Consequences

SIN is not a pleasant subject. Neither is leprosy.

I shall not soon forget one day, more than a dozen years ago, when a little party of those who had gone from America to attend the World's Sunday-school Convention at Jerusalem were passing out from the Holy City toward the Mount of Olives. I was at a little distance from my wife, when I saw a friend, who was near her, spring forward and put out his hand in front of her. A leper had just been reaching out and trying to attract her attention by laying hold of her arm. A heart-breaking sight—those lepers in our Lord's land were; hands and feet and even faces rotted away by the dread disease for which there is no human cure.

Suppose you went to an institution for the insane, or to a hospital for the incurable, and, looking upon these persons hopelessly in the bondage of mental or bodily disease, you asked, "Why are they in this awful condition?" and the answer came back, "They were born so."

This world as God sees it is a vast hospital, filled with human beings whose minds and bodies are diseased. Why? They were born so.

Why are men lost? They were born so. For "by one man sin entered into the world, and death by sin; and so death passed upon all men" (Rom. 5:12). All men are sinners by birth. Sin is what they have inherited.

See how God describes this congenital sinful nature of all of us. "The carnal mind," the apostle calls it. "For to be carnally minded is death; . . . because the carnal mind is enmity against God: for it is not subject to the law of God, neither indeed can be" (Rom. 8: 6, 7).

Looking back at our first human parents,—was Adam born sinful? No; he was created without sin; temptation was brought to him from without, he chose sin, down he went, and with him he dragged down the whole world,—with one stroke this earth and all mankind went into the bondage of sin.

Satan was the being who proposed to our first parents that they should sin. Was Satan created sinful? No; we are given glimpses in God's Word of the beauty and wisdom and power of this great spirit-being before he sinned, as in such a passage as Ezekiel 28:12-15,—"Thou wast perfect in thy ways from the day that thou wast created, till iniquity was found in thee." Then, "How art thou fallen from heaven, O Lucifer, son of the morning! how art thou cut down to the ground, which didst weaken the nations! For thou hast said in thine heart, I will ascend into heaven, I will exalt my throne above the stars of God: ... I will be like the most High. Yet thou shalt be brought down to hell, to the sides of the pit" (Isa. 14:12-15).

There was the beginning of sin in all the universe: when some one said, "I will," over against God's will. Sin is the opposite of God's will; sin is any variation from God's will. Sin wrecked Satan; sin wrecked the universe; sin wrecked man; sin wrecked the created and restored earth. And if we want to see the awful onworking and outworking of sin in man, we find the inspired record of its blackness and horrors in such a passage as Romans 1:28-32; and in the third chapter of that same great epistle, verses 9-18, where we find God saying, "There is none righteous, no, not one," with another terrible description of what sin and bondage mean.

Turning from Satan and Adam, every man knows that *he himself has sinned,* over and over again, in deliberate rejection and repudiation of God's will. "For all have sinned, and come short of the glory of God" (Rom. 3:23).

It does not take an honest man very long, in a study of his own life, to decide whether or not he has sinned. It does not take any exhaustive study of the world about us to decide whether or not the world is a sinful world. And it does not take an expert historian to examine the

11

records of history in order to come to a conclusion as to whether mankind's history has been saturated with sin. Even profane or secular history is clear as to this; and God's history of the world, in the Bible, unerringly shows that, from the time when Adam and Eve were created sinless until this present moment, all history has been made up of a succession of ages or dispensations, each one going down-hill in increasing sin until it reached such a depth of failure that God had to end that age, in judgment for its sin, and then give mankind a fresh opportunity by a new start. But with each new age the downgrade soon began again, till the age was ended in man's failure and God's judgment, this process only to be repeated again until we have come to the present day in the present age of grace, which God tells us will end, like all preceding ages, in failure.

Yes, the sin-story of man is a sad one. And the tragedy of it is that man left to himself would go on sinning forever. *Sin never cures itself.* Sin is not "a stumble upward." Sin is sin, and all sin is black sin,—so black, as Billy Sunday has said, that it would "make a black mark on a piece of anthracite." Sin is death. Sin is murder. Sin is suicide. Sin separates men from God. Sin destroys the spiritual life of man. *"In the day that thou eatest thereof thou shalt surely die,"* said God to Adam, warning him against the sin of disobedience (Gen. 2:17). And that very day

12

Sin and Its Consequences

Adam died spiritually, even as his body was to die later because of that sin.

Separated from God by sin, man not only loses the life of his spirit and of his body, but man cannot do right. He is a constant injury to others, he is a constant injury to himself. And the ending of it all is hell,—eternal separation from God and eternal punishment.

Many people have objected to Billy Sunday's preaching of hell. They forget that the Christ whom Billy Sunday offers to men as Saviour spoke the most terrible words about hell that can be found anywhere in the Bible.

Men are lost because of sin and its consequences, and because they are sinners. God makes this pleadingly plain to us. God wants no man to be lost; he would "have all men to be saved, and come unto the knowledge of the truth" (I Tim. 2:4). And "God so loved the world, that he gave his only begotten Son, that whosoever believeth on him should not perish, but have everlasting life" (John 3:16). He gave his best when he gave his only begotten Son. He exhausted all his resources when he let Jesus be crucified on the cross to pay the penalty of our sins. He went to the uttermost in the death of Christ; in time or eternity he can go no farther. And so those who do not believe on Jesus, who do not accept the salvation that is freely theirs through the death of Christ if they will but take it,—they are lost. "It is Jesus or hell."

II

How Men Are Saved

God's Part in Salvation

SUPPOSE you should step out on to the street, and there, standing on the curbstone, roll up your sleeves, take a knife, open an artery in your arm, and let the blood gush out into the gutter; what would be the result? The answer is simple: after enough of the blood had left your body you would drop over unconscious; and a very short time after that you would be dead.

That is exactly what has happened, spiritually, to every one who has ever done anything wrong in his life. Rather, it was done for him before he was born, when the father of the human race sinned and in that act of sin let the spiritual life of himself and of all mankind pour out until he and the race were "dead in trespasses and sins" (Eph. 2:1).

This answers our question of the previous chapter, "Why Men Are Lost." The man from whose physical body all the life-blood has poured out is a lost man, so far as his physical life is

15

concerned. The man from whose spirit the God-
life is gone is a lost man, so far as his spiritual
life is concerned. Sin separates us from the life
of God. Did you ever sin? Then, left to yourself, you are spiritually dead, a lost soul.

And how are you going to be saved?

A reader of The Sunday School Times recently
asked the question, "What do you consider the
most dangerous heresy today?"

What answer would you have made? Christian Science? New Thought? Russellism, or
Millennial Dawnism? Spiritualism,—or Spirit-
ism? The New Theology? The Higher Criti-
cism? All of these are dangerous enough!
Bloodless beliefs, almost all of them, leaving out
the cross of Christ and leading men away from
the only hope and way of life, to remain dead
and hopeless in their sins.

No; dangerous and deadly though all these
and other false religions of today are, there is
another heresy that may safely be called more
dangerous still, because it is abroad in the church
of Christ everywhere and among professing
Christians on every hand.

The most dangerous heresy of today is the
emphasis that is being made, within the church
itself and by Christian leaders and teachers and
ministers, upon activity as Christianity; upon
service as salvation.

16

God's Part in Salvation

Get busy for God, we are told, and your salvation will take care of itself. Serve your fellowmen, and don't worry about creeds. Forget your creeds and *do* something worth while. Activity as the way of life: that is the most dangerous heresy today. For *men are not saved by doing anything.*

Stop a minute, and look at that man whose arteries were opened, and whose blood has poured out from his body, lying there dead in the gutter. Would it be a hopeful thing to step up to him and say, "Just get up and do something, and you will be all right"?

Is a dead man going to be brought to life, saved, by *doing* something?

Or would the "kindly" counsel that his hope of "salvation," his life, lies in his activity for others, be only irony and mockery to him?

No; it is not Good News—and the Gospel is Good News—to tell a dead man that he must do something. It is not evangelism to offer a man advice that he cannot possibly accept. The "get busy" slogan is as devilish a delusion, when offered as the way of salvation, as to encourage a hospital ward full of incurable paralytics to believe that a little while spent in vigorous "setting up" exercises will make them sound and healthy human beings.

If the dead man is going to live, he will have to be brought to life. And the only one who can bring the dead to life is God. *God,* then, has got to do something about man's salvation. Man cannot do anything for his own salvation.

And God *has done it!*

That, praise God, is the Gospel! *That* is the Good News.

We cannot too often remind ourselves of the truth of the old saying, "Law says *do;* grace says *done."* The law saves no one, for "There is none righteous, no, not one" (Rom. 3:10) ; and it takes a righteous man to *do* the law of God. But grace, the grace of God, which gives to man, not requires from man, does for man that which man cannot do for himself.

God does not mock that wretched, sin-degraded, sin-destroyed dead man lying there in the gutter with no life in his veins. God would be mocking that man dead in trespasses and sins if He told him just to do the right thing and all would be well. No; God says lovingly, and in a voice that even the dead can hear, "I have done it all for you; will you accept this?"

What is it that God has done?

When, through Adam's fall, mankind sinned and the whole human race went down into ruin, there were three things we can think of that God might do.

He might ignore man's sin, and, himself a perfect, sinless, and holy God, take into fellowship with himself for time and eternity sinful, sinning, sin-saturated human beings. But that is inconceivable. A holy, sinless God *cannot* ignore sin.

Well, then, God might let all men for time and eternity receive the full, inevitable consequences of their sin, thereby being forever separated and cut off from fellowship with Him. Thus all human beings would go to hell, forever lost. This also is unthinkable; God did not create the human race in his own image to have that race, in its entirety, forever lost.

There is only one other possibility. God cannot ignore sin; and God cannot ignore man. Then God himself must pay the penalty of man's sin in order that man may be saved, while at the same time sin is taken fully into account and dealt with as the black, heinous fact that it is.

God *cannot* condone sin; he *must* condemn it. The wages of sin is death; and God cannot set aside or abrogate those wages while he continues to be a holy and righteous God. If only a single member of the human race is to be saved from paying the death penalty of sin, God must pay that penalty himself. And that is the necessity for the death of Christ. His death indeed showed forth the supreme love of God for men. But we see that it did infinitely more.

In our human way we may, as it were, think of the members of the Godhead, far back in the infinite reaches of eternity, before ever creation had begun, holding a loving council together over the question of how man's coming sin should be dealt with while man himself should be saved. And we can, as it were, see the only and eternal Son of God, loving that Father as no human child ever loved a parent, and loved by that Father as no human parent ever loved a child, agreeing with the Father to take the place of sinning, sinful man in order that God's holy and necessary wrath against sin might be visited to the needed uttermost upon—not sinful man, but the sinless Son of man standing in sinful man's place. Such a plan, agreed upon by the Godhead in the councils of eternity, meant such a heart-break of sorrow in the Godhead as no man can conceive. No human father or mother, giving their only son in this black hour of world war as their sacrifice to their nation, knows the meaning of heart-break as God the Father knew it when he gave his only begotten Son. No human son, loving his human father in the most perfect love known to the heart of man, and knowing that he is to be separated from that father for all of life-time, knows anything of the heart-break of the Son as he, for our sakes and in our stead, was separated from the loving heart of his heavenly Father.

The plan agreed upon by the Father and the Son and the Holy Spirit in the councils of eternity was, in the fulness of time, consummated. God the Son, "being in the form of God, thought it not robbery to be equal with God: but made himself of no reputation, and took upon him the form of a servant, and was made in the likeness of men: and being found in fashion as a man, he humbled himself, and became obedient unto death, even the death of the cross" (Phil. 2:6-8).

And not only did God thus become man, continuing to be God while also he was man; but he, sinless, actually *became sin* for our sakes. "For he hath made him to be sin for us, who knew no sin" (II Cor. 5:21). Thus becoming actually our sin, in a way that we cannot understand but that we can and must literally accept unless we are to make God a liar (I John 5:10), the sinless Christ, because he had become sin, became actually a curse in the sight of God. For sin is a loathsome, accursed thing in God's sight; and it always must be so while God is God. Jesus Christ, "the Lamb of God, which taketh away the sin of the world" (John 1:29) was nailed to the cross and actually hung there, in his voluntarily accepted human body of humiliation, despised by men and accursed in the sight of the Father. He had really been "made a curse for us; for it is written, Cursed is every one that hangeth on a tree" (Gal. 3:13). God could not look in loving fellowship upon this supreme gathering together there, in that broken, bleeding human body, of the sin of all mankind. God, because he *is* sinless and holy and eternally hating the sin that destroys men and would if it could destroy God, must turn away his face from the Lamb hanging there "who his own self bare our sins in his own body on the tree" (I Peter 2:24); and, for the first time in eternity, the Father turned away his face from his only Son.

It had to be so. Sin separates from God. The Son of God, having become the sin of the world, was separated from the Father. The black horror of that tragedy staggers our minds; we cannot conceive it. And then came the heart-broken, agonizing cry of time and eternity: *"My God, my God, why hast thou forsaken me?"*

We know the answer—God's answer. He had turned away from his only begotten Son, made to be sin on our behalf, that he might visit upon him the wrath that must otherwise fall upon us. In order that we might be spared, God "spared not his own Son, but delivered him up for us all" (Rom. 8:32).

And so the blow fell. God had struck; struck at the most hateful thing in the universe, sin; struck at the sin of all mankind as God must do because he is holy and loving. But that sin of all mankind was there in the body and person of his only Son!

Nineteen centuries before this blackest day in history another loving father and another loving son were together at the place of sacrifice. God was showing men, nineteen hundred years before it occurred, the meaning of Calvary. Acting in heart-broken obedience to the will of God, "Abraham stretched forth his hand, and took the knife to slay his son." Yet in that awful moment, when his son's life trembled in the balance, "the angel of the Lord called unto him out of heaven, and said, Abraham, Abraham." Then came the loving command from God, "Lay not thine hand upon the lad, neither do thou any thing unto him: for now I know that thou fearest God, seeing thou hast not withheld thy son, *thine only son* from me." And Abraham took the little animal that was there at hand, provided by God, "and offered him up for a burnt offering in the stead of his son."

But this day on Calvary, as God's hand was raised to strike the body of his Son, *his only Son,* there was no one to stay his hand. And so the blow fell; and Jesus died. The necessary, righteous, loving wrath of God against the sin that would destroy God's children was visited in full upon that only Son who hung there in the sinner's place.

It has been said, and truly, that God never strikes twice for the same sin. The penalty of the sin of all mankind had been paid. "As by the offence of one judgment came upon all men to condemnation; even so by the righteousness of one the free gift came upon all men unto justification of life" (Rom. 5:18). All men for all time were free from the condemnation of sin.

Free, that is, if they would accept God's unspeakable gift. The freedom was there for the taking, for the believing; but it was never to be forced upon them. Since the Lamb of God took away the sin of the world men go to hell, not because they are sinners, but because they will not accept God's freely offered pardon of their sin, purchased for them by the only begotten Son of God at such terrible cost to the Father and the Son.

This, then, is the meaning of the death of Christ. This is why the supreme mission of Christ was, not his LIFE here on earth, but his DEATH here on earth. Not because he lived, but because he died, we may live—if we accept the result of his death. Believers are "reconciled to God by the death of his Son" (Rom. 5:10). This is why all eternity looked forward, and all eternity will continue to look backward, to the death of Jesus Christ as the supremest redemptive moment in the history of God and man.

That is what God has *done* for us dead men. He let his only begotten Son die as our Substitute, die in our place and for our sins, receiving in himself the full penalty that we deserve to receive because of our sins. And then, having been delivered "for our offences," that Son "was raised again for our justification" (Rom. 4:25).

Do you believe it? God is telling us this wonderful Good News, telling it in tones that can awaken even the hearing of the dead: that he has

God's Part in Salvation

done it all, and if we will but believe, he, by the finished work of that crucified, raised, and ascended Son, will raise us from the dead, give us new life in his Son Christ Jesus, and we shall be saved.

May the Holy Spirit make new to us all, with the unsearchable riches of the love of God, the meaning of the marvelous Good News, that "God so loved the world, that he gave his only begotten Son, that whosoever believeth in him should not perish, but have everlasting life."

Will you accept the Father's unspeakable gift of his Son as your Substitute and your Saviour? *Do* you so accept him? If you do, tell him so now.

The substance of this chapter, from pages 18 to 25, may be had as a separate pamphlet, entitled, "Was Jesus' Life or Death the More Important?" It is published by The Sunday-School Times Company, Philadelphia, at 20 cents a dozen copies; fifty or more, one cent each; single copies, 2 cents each, postpaid.

III

How Men Are Saved

Man's Part in Salvation

A FRIEND of mine, who is a young business man, recently asked twenty-five different Sunday-school teachers in Philadelphia if they knew whether they were saved. Twenty-three of the twenty-five did not know. And they are—or they are supposed to be—teaching others the way of salvation!

Suppose you were walking along the street and a stranger stepped up to you and asked if you could tell him how to get to a certain place. Suppose your reply was, "Come with me." And then, when the stranger asked, "Are you going there yourself?" suppose you replied, "I don't know." What would the stranger think of you as a dependable guide?

Perhaps those twenty-three "agnostic" Sunday-school teachers ("agnostic," you remember, means "I don't know") are not sure whether they have done their part in being saved.

What is man's part in salvation? We saw in the preceding chapter what is God's part.

Do you remember the story of the man who was lost in a snowstorm in the mountains? He pushed on his way, hoping against hope; finally his strength began to fail, and the darkness came on, and before long he realized that he could not go much farther. When he was about to drop down in exhaustion, knowing full well that if he did so he would never get up again, he stumbled against something, and leaning over and brushing away the snow he found that it was another man, lying there unconscious. Eagerly he sought to bring this man back to consciousness; and he succeeded. Then he got him to sit up, then to kneel, then on to his feet, then to walk a few steps; and now he urged the man to keep moving as he valued his life. Together they forced their way through the blinding snowstorm; finally they saw a light ahead, staggered into the house from which it came, and *both* were saved.

The point of that story is: if you want salvation, go out and do something for somebody else. You will save yourself by forgetting yourself and saving others.

Don't ever tell that story, in an evangelistic message, as an illustration of the Gospel. If you do, you will be lying. We could not have a better illustration of what the Gospel is not. No soul, since Adam sinned, has ever saved himself that way—by saving another.

Let us set it down, then, that *service is not salvation.* Man's part in salvation is *not* to serve others.

Trying to serve others spiritually, without a Saviour, and finding that we cannot be of any spiritual service to them, may indeed force us into the realization that we and they need a Saviour. One of the greatest Christian leaders of our generation says that he came to believe in the deity of Christ in just that way; he was doing work among men in prison, and he found that those men needed supernatural help, help that he could not possibly give them, and so he was driven to accept the deity of Christ.

Turning over a new leaf is *not* man's part in salvation. That is, a man does not get saved by reforming, by saying "I will clean up my life, and take a new start." For man gets saved only by a Saviour; and if he could clean up his life himself he would need no Saviour.

Some years ago, when a certain group of Unitarian churches in Boston were doing special work together, they asked a Methodist Episcopal church to be responsible for the people in a section of the city which included some of the lowest slums. They decided that the Methodists had better take charge of the rescue work there; for somehow, said the Unitarians, the Methodists seemed to reach those who were lowest down more effectively; they could bring these "down and outs" up to a certain point, and then the Unitarians could take hold and help.

Exactly! The evangelical believers, counting upon Christ as Saviour, could reach those whom "liberal" workers, appealing only to men to clean up and reform themselves, could never reach. What an unconscious tribute of the hopeless "Gospel" of "salvation by character" to the true Gospel of character by salvation!

Asserting one's manhood is *not* man's part in salvation. If a man would be saved, the first thing he is to do is not to "be a man." Yet we often hear the appeal for Christ made in that mistaken way.

An evangelist who preaches the true Gospel, who is true to the shed blood of Jesus, and whose work God has abundantly honored in using him to bring thousands to salvation through personal faith in Christ as Saviour, nevertheless often puts a regrettable emphasis upon the mistaken appeal to the unsaved. "Be a man, not a mutt or a molly-coddle!" "Hit the trail and show your manhood!" is the cry. "Hold up your head, throw back your shoulders, look the world straight in the eye, and make your decision for Christ."

These and other such appeals are constantly heard, even in true evangelistic work; the emphasis being upon the idea that man's part in salvation is to do the strong thing instead of the weak thing; do right and stop doing wrong; prove his manhood by enlisting on the side of righteousness; and so on. But that is not the Gospel. That is not the way of salvation. That is not man's part in salvation.

Thinking back for a moment to that man who was discussed in the preceding chapter, whose arteries were opened, whose life-blood had poured out, and who was lying dead in the gutter, —is his part in salvation to assert his manhood? To lift up his head, throw back his shoulders, step forward and enlist in the cause of righteousness? No: dead men cannot do that.

The cross of Christ does not call upon men to assert their manhood. The cross of Christ exposes men's degradation. That is part of "the offence of the cross" (Gal. 5:11); it does not appeal to the natural man's pride; it unsparingly shows him that he cannot do anything for himself; that he has no manhood, no righteousness, no decency to offer God.

Right thinking is *not* man's part in salvation. New Thought would tell us that it is. Concentrate your mind on all that is clean, and true, and pure, and good, and holy, says New Thought, and you will be saved,—rather, you will save yourself, for "the divine spark" is within you, and needs only to be cultivated. Keep a picture of your mother, or your wife, or your sister or sweetheart, in your watch, and look at it frequently.

Think high thoughts. This "right thinking" plan of salvation even quotes Scripture to a man, and says, "Whatsoever things are true, whatsoever things are honest, . . . whatsoever things are of good report . . . think on these things," and your salvation will take care of itself. Those who would pervert and misuse God's Word in this way fail to mention the fact that that passage of Scripture is addressed, not to those who would be saved, but to those who, through faith in Jesus Christ as Saviour and in his shed blood and finished work on Calvary, already *have been saved*. The verse begins with the words, "Finally, brethren"; and "brethren" means believers. Men cannot be saved by thinking right.

Man's part in salvation is *not* to *deny the existence of sin*. Another false religion tells him to do so. Deny sin, says Christian Science, and it will not bother you. Suppose the Allied Armies simply denied the existence of the German armies for a while, and took up their daily life as though Germans and German armies did not exist. How soon would victory come to the Allies!

No, salvation does not come by any such suicidal insanity as the denial of the existence of sin. God does not deny the existence of sin; he declares it in words of righteous wrath and indignation, and in expression of his eternal enmity against this terrible reality, Sin. The cross of Christ the Son of God is God's recognition of sin. "The Lord hath laid on him the iniquity of us all" (Isa. 53:6). "But the scripture hath concluded all under sin" (Gal. 3:22). One of the first steps for man to take, for his salvation, is not to deny but to recognize his sin.

To *deny self* is *not* man's part in salvation. Many an ascetic has thought that it is. In heathen lands and in Christian lands we see men vainly trying to save themselves by attempting to crucify self, put self to death. Is a thing desirable to them naturally?—they give it up. Is a thing hard to do?—they do it. But no one ever has been, and no one ever will be, saved that way. After we have been saved, it is, indeed, a duty and a privilege to deny self,—the self that was crucified with Christ on the cross. But this denial of self is not a condition of salvation, it is a result of salvation. And even the Christian's denial of self is possible only by faith in Christ for this: letting Christ put to death that self which we can never put to death for ourselves.

Finally, even *sacrifice* is *not* man's part in salvation. The utter sacrifice of himself will save no man. Let us keep clear on this, in these days of sacrificial living and sacrificial giving and sacrificial dying because of the world war. The sacrifices that are being so lavishly, unreservedly made now, on both sides of the Atlantic, to win this war against the forces of unrighteousness are blessed to see, and we may well thank God for them. Both the world and the church are being taught lessons in sacrifice to an extent never seen before. But may God defend us from the subtle and devilish plausibility of the lie, which has been preached even in some so-called Christian pulpits, that the soldier who lays down his life on the battlefield in the cause of the Allies is, by that sacrificial act, assured of going straight to heaven.

Some few soldiers may believe this; some are writing magazine articles in which the untruth is declared that the discipline and sacrifice of soldier life in this awful struggle cleanses a man from all sin and atones for any past wrong in his life, squaring him with God, so that he can face God fearlessly. But there are plenty of soldiers who are not deceived by this. They are keen enough to see and to say, as some one has pointed out, that this battlefield-death-salvation theory would give more efficacy to a German bullet than to the blood of Christ.

No, sacrifice is not the way of salvation, though it may be a blessed result of salvation. But, says some one, did not our Lord Jesus himself say, "Greater love hath no man than this, that a man lay down his life for his friends" (John 15:13)? Yes, our Lord said that. But he nowhere said that the man who lays down his life for his friends wins his salvation in that way. Sacrifice is one thing; salvation is another; and the Word of God never confuses them, though men often

34

do. There is a specious appeal in that favorite bit of characteristic American verse, "Jim Bludso," the godless, blasphemous, adulterous engineer of a Mississippi steamboat who, one night when his steamer took fire, held her bow against the river bank until every last soul was safe ashore, while Jim himself gave up his life on the burning boat; and the moral of it all is this, that

> "He seen his duty, a dead sure thing,—
>   And went for it thar and then;
> And Christ ain't agoing to be too hard
>   On a man that died for men."

It is very appealing to the natural pride of the unsaved man, but even Jim Bludso's death is not sufficient to set aside God's Word and make God a liar.

A Christian woman said the other day to a friend that she had a pet conviction of her own, though she said she knew it was not Scriptural: it was that a good many lovely, unselfish people whom she knew, but who have no use for religion, were going to get into heaven in some way, so there must be some "side-door" for them. There have been times when all of us would like to have been able to believe that, for the sake of some one we have known. But God knows that it is not possible; and he has made this very plain. There is no side-door to heaven. There is only one door, and that is Christ. "I am the door," said he; "by me if any man enter in, he shall be saved." And he had just said, "Verily, verily, I say unto you, He that entereth not by the door into the sheepfold, but climbeth up some other way, the same is a thief and a robber,"—and heaven is a place "where thieves do not break through" (Matt. 6:20; John 10:1-9). There is only one way into heaven: "Jesus saith unto him, I am the way, . . . no man cometh unto the Father, but by me" (John 14:6). "Neither is there salvation in any other: for there is none other name under heaven given among men, whereby we must be saved" (Acts 4:12).

Why is it that none of those seven ways, nor all of them together, will save a man: service, reformation, being a man, right thinking, denying the existence of sin, denying self, and sacrifice?

Well, one reason is that no one could ever do any of these things *perfectly*. And to be completely or perfectly saved requires that the work of salvation be done perfectly. You remember the story of the farmer who prided himself on his morality, and who, when pleaded with to accept Christ as Saviour, always replied that he was doing pretty well as he was. One day he employed a man to build a fence around his farm, and went out to see how the work was getting on.

"Is the fence good and strong?" the farmer asked.

"It's a good average fence," answered the man; "there are one or two gaps, but I will have made up for those by doubling the rails on each side of the gaps."

"What!" exclaimed the farmer, "do you mean to tell me that you have built a fence with gaps in it? Don't you know that if a fence is not perfect it is worthless?"

"I used to think so," said the man; "but I hear you talking so much about averaging matters with the Lord that it seemed to me we might try it with the cattle."

A "good average" will not fool either the Lord or cattle.

"For whosoever shall keep the whole law, and yet offend in one point, he is guilty of all" (James 2:10).

But there is One who has kept the whole law, not offending in one point. He, and he only, can accomplish salvation for sinful men.

Salvation is something that must be won *for* us; it never can be won *by* us. That is what we mean when we say that salvation is by grace, not by works; by the grace of God for men, not by the works of men for God.

Salvation is a substitutionary thing. It is won for sinful men by Another becoming their Substitute. In the substitionary death of Christ on the cross he died for the sins of the world. We saw in the last chapter how this was so, and why it was necessary. The death penalty of man's sin has been paid, forever and completely.

What, then, is man's part in salvation? It is just to *believe* that the thing has been done. When Jesus Christ died for men's sins, was raised from the dead, ascended into heaven and sent his Holy Spirit to this earth, the way was open for God to save every sinner who—what? Who would serve Him perfectly? Who would assert his manhood? Who would live a sacrificial life? No; the way was open for God to save every sinner who *believes* that *God has done it all!* For "God so loved the world, that he gave his only begotten Son, that whosoever believeth in him should not perish, but have everlasting life" (John 3:16). It is man's part simply to decide whether God is speaking the truth or is lying. For the man who deliberately decides that God is a liar, God can do nothing more.

✶ Man's part in salvation is to do nothing, but let God do it all. There is just one passage in the whole Bible that says that man can in any way work for his salvation. Jesus spoke the words. He had been talking to the Jews about laboring "not for the meat which perisheth, but for that meat which endureth unto everlasting life, which the Son of man shall give unto you." They asked him how they could "work the works of God."

Man's Part in Salvation

Listen to our Lord's reply: "This is the work of God, that *ye believe on him whom he hath sent*" (John 6: 27-29).✶

In other words, the only saving work that man can do is—believe.

The Bible never contradicts itself; so we find the Holy Spirit saying through Paul, "To him that worketh not, but believeth on him that justifieth the ungodly, his faith is counted for righteousness" (Rom. 4: 5).

And again, "Believe on the Lord Jesus Christ, and thou shalt be saved" (Acts 16: 31).

What *is* belief? do you ask? What is the faith that is necessary to salvation?

It is the simplest thing in the world. "Faith does nothing; faith lets God do it all." Faith just faces the facts, and recognizes that they are facts, and accepts them for oneself. And could we have any better evidence that certain alleged facts *are* facts than to hear God saying that they are facts? This is what makes the Bible so substantial and comforting. It is God settling the facts for us, that we may believe and be saved.

✶How are we going to have faith, the faith we need for salvation?✶ Just look into the Word of God and see what he says about the way of salvation. "So then faith cometh by hearing, and hearing by the word of God" (Rom. 10: 17).

39

Faith feeds on facts; and the blessedest facts in the universe are the facts of what Christ has done.

If you want a great faith, face great facts. The greatest Fact of all is Christ. "And I," he said, "if I be lifted up from the earth, will draw all men unto me" (John 12 : 32). "And as Moses lifted up the serpent in the wilderness, even so must the Son of man be lifted up: That whosoever believeth in him should not perish, but have eternal life" (John 3 :14, 15).

Let us give men the facts, and trust God to do the rest.

IV

WHAT IS SALVATION?

Past, Present, and Future

MAY God keep us from ever saying, with a look of pious humility, "I *trust* that I am saved!" Of those twenty-three out of twenty-five Sunday-school teachers, mentioned in the last chapter, who did not know whether or not they were saved, doubtless some *hoped* that they were. But the believer in Jesus Christ has no business to hope that he is saved. Hope looks toward the future, and it has a very blessed place in our salvation, as we shall see later. But our salvation is also of the present, and of the past; and it is the Christian's duty and privilege to *know* that he is saved. The Christian who only hopes that he is saved is hoping that God is not a liar,—whether he says it in this shockingly frank way or not. The Christian who knows that God's Word is true has the privilege and the duty of knowing that he is saved. Jesus said, on the cross, "It is finished" (John 19:30). God says that he raised Jesus from the dead for our justification (Rom. 4:25). Our Lord himself says, "Verily, verily, I say unto you, He that heareth

41

my word, and believeth on him that sent me, *hath* everlasting life, and shall not come into condemnation; but *is* passed from death unto life" (John 5:24). That settles it. I believe on Jesus. I know that I am saved. Because God says so. And I believe him. "For I know whom I have believed, and am persuaded that he is able to keep that which I have committed unto him against that day" (II Tim. 1:12).

Dr. J. Wilbur Chapman tells of a period of doubt that he had in his own Christian life, years ago, when he was not sure whether he was saved, and could not seem to get clear on it. He told Mr. Moody one day that for some reason or other he could not seem to believe.

Moody wheeled sharply around upon him. *"Whom can't you believe?"* he demanded.

And Chapman saw the point. He had been saying that, "somehow," he could not believe God! Now he saw that he *could* believe God. He saw that he could not disbelieve God. And he rested thankfully in the *fact* of his salvation.

Some years ago I was talking with a Christian man who rather prided himself on being of a scientific and investigating turn of mind. "What do *you* mean by 'being saved'?" he asked me. I answered in a somewhat hesitating and cautious way, saying something about salvation as being eternal fellowship with God, and being "lost" as meaning eternal separation from God. Well, that is true, but if I were asked that question to-day I should not try to tone down anything. When a man is saved he is saved *from* going to hell; and he is saved *to* going to heaven.

One of the strongest Christian leaders of our generation said to me, after the Billy Sunday campaign in Philadelphia in 1915, that one of the outstanding lessons he had learned from that campaign was this: he was now going to talk about hell more than he had been doing.

"Oh, but men aren't frightened into the king-dom of heaven," says some one. That is a devil-ishly clever lie. Men *are* frightened into turning from their sins and seeking a way of escape from hell and the pains of hell which they know is the end of the sinner who does not find some way of escape. At any rate, Jesus seemed to believe that fear played a very important part in the message that he came from heaven to earth to bring to men. John the Baptist, under the in-spiration of the Holy Spirit, seemed to think so. The Holy Spirit himself, in the writing of the Bible and in the directing of God's prophets and messengers, seems to think so. And God's method is a safe one for us to use,—until we find a better.

It was not Billy Sunday, but John the Baptist, who flamed out, "O generation of vipers, who hath warned you to flee from the wrath to come? Bring forth therefore fruits meet for repentance: . . . And now also the ax is laid unto the root of the trees: therefore every tree which bringeth not forth good fruit is hewn down, and cast into the fire. I indeed baptize you with water unto repentance: but he that cometh after me is mightier than I, whose shoes I am not worthy to bear: he shall baptize you with the Holy Ghost, and with fire: Whose fan is in his hand, and he will throughly purge his floor, and gather his wheat into the garner; but he will burn up the chaff with unquenchable fire" (Matt. 3:7-12).

Have you made a special study of what the New Testament says about hell? Every one who would tell men the Good News of Jesus Christ ought to do so. For what makes the Good News so good is its shining contrast with the blackness and hopelessness of the world and mankind without the Good News.

See what our Lord himself says about hell, for example,—and remember that the most terrible words about hell come from the lips of Christ himself,—in Mark 9:40-48, as he declares that any cost, such as cutting off the hand or the foot, or plucking out the eye, is better than to be "cast into hell fire: Where their worm dieth not, and the fire is not quenched." Read his account of the torments of the rich man after death, vainly asking that Lazarus might "dip the tip of his finger in water, and cool my tongue; for I am tormented in this flame"; and then the terrible reply from paradise that this cannot be, because "between us and you there is a great gulf fixed: so that they which would pass from hence to you cannot; neither can they pass to us, that would come from thence" (Luke 16:19-31).

See what is said of the fate of those who, at the coming of Christ, are found knowing not God, nor obeying the Gospel of our Lord Jesus Christ, when the Lord Jesus himself comes "in flaming fire taking vengeance on them . . . who shall be punished with everlasting destruction from the presence of the Lord, and from the glory of his power" (II Thess. 1:7-9).

And in the last book of the entire Bible, almost at the end of that book, when the glorified Christ has unveiled to his beloved apostle things that are to come, he not only says that "the devil that deceived them was cast into the lake of fire and brimstone, where the beast and the false prophet are, and shall be tormented day and night for ever and ever," but also that at the "great white throne" of judgment before God, "whosoever was not found written in the book of life was cast into the lake of fire" (Rev. 20:10-15).

Do you *believe* what God says about hell? Two Christian men were talking about this recently, and as the awfulness and unspeakable tragedy of it swept over their souls, they both said to each other that it made them feel that they must go out on the streets then and there and preach Christ to men.

Is it an accident that the greatest soul-winners believe in hell, and also believe in a Christ who can save from hell?

We have a threefold salvation: For the past, the present, and the future.

Our salvation for the past is that, through the substitutionary death of Christ on the cross, in our stead and place, we are saved from the *penalty* of our sins.

. That work of salvation was finished nineteen centuries ago. It was done then, all done, done so perfectly and completely that God is absolutely satisfied with it, and will be through time and eternity. Nothing that man or God can ever do will or can add anything to the completion, the perfection, of the salvation there wrought.

God showed that he was satisfied with what his Son Jesus had done on the cross when he raised the dead body of that Son, lying cold and lifeless and helpless in the tomb, to life again.

And in view of the perfect and complete work that the Son of God did in paying the penalty of the sins of the world, have you realized that, ever since that time, no sinner, no unsaved person, need ever or ought ever to make the prayer, "God be merciful to me a sinner"? Such a prayer is an insult to God. Why?

46

Past, Present, and Future

Because God, from that day to this, has been telling the world of unsaved sinners that he *was* merciful to them all when he gave his only begotten Son to die in their place and to receive in himself the penalty that they deserved. *That* was the mercy of God: giving us "the unspeakable gift" (II Cor. 9:15).

Suppose I owe you a million dollars; and there is no hope of my paying you. Suppose a friend pays this debt for me, and you accept the payment and give him a receipt in full. Suppose I am told that the debt is paid, and that I am completely free from all obligation in the matter. And then suppose I ask you for mercy, plead with you to be merciful to me in this matter. Wouldn't it be an insult? Would I not be showing that I feared that you, although paid in full, were the sort of person who would yet try to take some advantage of me in this matter? Now God, against whom all our sin is committed, and who therefore is the one to whom the world owes its unspeakable, unpayable debt for sin, accepted the payment of Jesus Christ, *and he gave a receipt in full when he raised him from the dead.* That was God's declaration that he was satisfied with the payment, satisfied with the perfect work that Christ had done. For he "raised up Jesus our Lord from the dead; who was delivered for our offences, and was raised again for our justification" (Rom. 4:24, 25).

We need not fear that God is going to ask for payment twice for the same debt. We need not ask God to be merciful to us because we are sinners. God does not want us to do that. He wants us to thank him for the gift of his Son whereby our debt was paid; he wants us to accept the mercy that he so freely offers in the death of Christ. When we do this, when by simple faith we accept Jesus as our Saviour, the debt is perfectly paid in our case,—the payment is so perfect that God cannot add anything to it. Our salvation then is in the past.

That is our Justification.

But there is a present salvation also that we need. Our justification gives us freedom from the *penalty* of our sin, that death-penalty which is hell. Meantime we go on living, under constant temptation, and we need a deliverance from the *power* of sin. Does our salvation include this?

Praise God, it does. But many a Christian does not know it.

Suppose you were one of a prisonful of convicted criminals, all sentenced to hard labor for a long term of years, then to have their lives ended by the death-penalty of the electric chair. Not a pleasant outlook, for either the present or the future. But just that is the outlook for the unsaved man. "The way of the transgressor is hard" (Prov. 13:15); and the end is hell. But suppose, while you were one of the convicted criminals in this prison, you were told that you had been pardoned from the death-penalty, while at the same time you stayed on in the prison at hard labor. That is the condition of many a Christian. He knows that he is saved from the eternal death-penalty of his sins. But, oh, the bondage of sin in the meantime! And there is no more reason for the Christian living on in the bondage of sin than there would be for any prisoner remaining at hard labor in that prison if a full and free pardon had been issued to all there, not only from the death-penalty, but also from labor and imprisonment of any sort. The thing to do then would be to walk out at once, free.

Dr. C. I. Scofield tells of a Mississippi woman whose family, at the time of the Civil War, had a large plantation and many negro slaves; and who one day called her slaves together and said, "You are free. The North has conquered, and the Proclamation of Emancipation has been issued by the President, and you are all free." It took her a week to get any of those slaves to believe it. Finally it got to them from other sources, and they began to believe that it was so, that they were really free.

Were they any freer, in reality, at the end of that week than at the beginning? Did Lincoln then add anything to their freedom?

Were the best workers, the most moral slaves on that plantation, any freer, after the emancipation came, than the lowest-down, most shiftless, worthless slaves?

No; all were equally free: for none were free because of what they had been or done, but because of the freedom that another had given.

Now listen to what God says about the freedom of the Christian:

"My little children, these things write I unto you that ye may not sin. Sin shall not have dominion over you: for ye are not under law [which says *do*], but under grace [which says *done*]. My grace is sufficient for thee: for my power is made perfect in weakness. Wherefore also he is able to save to the uttermost [or, completely] them that draw near unto God through him, seeing he ever liveth to make intercession for them. There hath no temptation taken you but such as man can bear: but God is faithful, who will not suffer you to be tempted above that ye are able; but will with the temptation make also the way of escape, that ye may be able to endure it. I can do all things through Christ which strengtheneth me. Thou shalt call his name JESUS; for it is he that shall save his people from their sins—that ye may become blameless and harmless, children of God without blemish in the midst of a crooked and perverse generation, among whom ye are seen as lights in the world.

Past, Present, and Future

Now unto him that is able to guard you from stumbling! Thanks be unto God, who always leadeth us in triumph in Christ! Our old man was crucified with him, that the body of sin might be done away, that so we should no longer be in bondage to sin; for he that hath died is released from sin. As therefore ye received Christ Jesus the Lord, so walk in him. For by grace have ye been saved through faith; and that not of yourselves, it is the gift of God; not of works, that no man should glory.'" (I John 2:1; Rom. 6:14; II Cor. 12:9; Heb. 7:25; I Cor. 10:13; Phil. 4:13; Matt. 1:21; Phil. 2:15; Jude 24; II Cor. 2:14; Rom. 6:6, 7; Col. 2:6; Eph. 2:8, 9).

Yes, God offers us in Jesus Christ a present salvation, freedom from the power of sin. This is our Sanctification. As some one has well said, we are separated *from* sin, and we are separated *to* God.

Our salvation is complete, yet our salvation is not complete. Our salvation from the penalty of sin is unimprovably perfect and complete, finished and past. Our salvation from the power of sin is complete moment by moment as we trust moment by moment in the sufficiency of Christ for this. Yet we still have the possibility of sinning; we are still living in sin-injured bodies,

---

¹ The text of these passages as here quoted is from the American Standard Version of the Bible, Copyright, 1901, by Thomas Nelson & Sons, to insure purity of text.

subject to sin, disease, and death. Is there no salvation from this?

Yes, praise God; we have a future salvation, which is to be ours at the coming of Christ. That is the "hope" part of our salvation, the forward look, the "blessed hope" that is taken up more fully in the next chapter.

In this future part of our salvation we are to be delivered from the very possibility of sinning. Our future salvation is "the glory which shall be revealed in us. For the earnest expectation of the creation waiteth for the manifestation of the sons of God . . . because the creation itself also shall be delivered from the bondage of corruption into the glorious liberty of the children of God." Meantime we are "waiting for the adoption, to wit, the redemption of our body" (Rom. 8:18-23).

We have a glorious salvation now; we are to have a still more glorious salvation. "Beloved, now are we the sons of God, and it doth not yet appear what we shall be: but we know that, when he shall appear, we shall be like him; for we shall see him as he is" (I John 3:2).

What is it, then, that is going to complete our salvation? Not death—death is an enemy, "the last enemy that shall be destroyed" (I Cor. 15:26). Through death, it is true, the believer passes into the presence of the Lord, and into wonderful joy and blessedness (Phil. 1:21-23).

Past, Present, and Future

But those who have already died in Christ, saved through faith in him, and who are in his presence today, are still looking forward to the future part of their salvation. It will be theirs, and ours, when Christ comes again. *Then* it is that these bodies of corruption will be changed and raised incorruptible. Then it is that death will be swallowed up in victory (I Cor. 15:52-54). Then it is that Christ himself shall appear, and the "blessed hope" be fulfilled. This is our Glorification.

These are the wonderful facts included for us in the salvation we have in Christ Jesus, for our past, our present, and our future. This is the Good News of our deliverance, through Christ, from the Penalty, the Power, the Presence and Possibility of sin.

A remarkable passage in the New Testament sums up this threefold salvation of the believer, for past, present, and future, in these words: "For the grace of God that bringeth salvation hath appeared to all men [in the past, when Jesus died for our sins], teaching us that, denying ungodliness and worldly lusts, we should live soberly, righteously, and godly, in this present world [that all may see that we have a present salvation from the power of sin]; looking for that blessed hope, and the glorious appearing of the great God and our Saviour Jesus Christ" (Tit. 2:11-13).

Are we praising God for these three great facts of our salvation?

Are we telling others, everywhere, in season and out of season, of the threefold Good News which God has for them through Jesus Christ?

V

SALVATION'S FORWARD LOOK

The Blessed Hope

HAS the truth of our Lord's return properly a place in a series of simple messages on the Gospel? Should it be brought into the evangelistic appeal to "the man in the street"?

Ask Paul, or Peter, or James, or John. Ask "the man in the street" himself what he knows about the Lord's return, and whether he would like to know more about it.

Not only has the truth of Christ's second coming a larger place in the New Testament than any other doctrine there, but the present world war has turned the attention of people everywhere to this truth as never before in the history of the world. It is our golden opportunity to tell of the "Blessed Hope," and to get a hearing for it that will gladden the heart of the evangelist and of our Lord himself.

A business man who had no special interest in religion or the Bible was in the office of a Christian lawyer in Philadelphia, not long ago, discussing the details of a business matter they had in hand. As they finished their conference, the conversation turned to the tragic war that is convulsing the world. "I don't know what you think about it," said the business man, "but it seems to me that things are in such hopeless chaos now that nothing can ever straighten them out short of God Almighty himself coming down to this earth and doing the job."

"You struck the nail on the head that time," answered the lawyer, who happened to be not only a real Christian but one who is looking for and loves the appearing of the Lord "That is exactly what is needed; and that is exactly what the Bible says God is going to do about it."

"What do you mean?" asked the friend, in surprise.

Then the Christian man had his opportunity; and in a few minutes he told his unbelieving friend some of the facts about Christ's coming back to this earth, with all that this shall mean to believers, and to unbelievers, and to the world in general.

"Take this little book along with you, and read it if you get a chance; it will tell you more about this wonderful truth," said the lawyer as his friend was leaving; and he handed him a book on the truth of our Lord's return.

A little later the business man, who had had no interest in religion or the Bible, came back to his lawyer friend and wanted to know more about the new line of truth on which he had been started. Gladly further help was given; and it was not long before that irreligious, unbelieving man had seen the way of salvation through the death of Christ his Saviour, and had taken that Saviour into his own heart, by simple faith, that he might be ready for Him when He should come.

Jesus is coming! Oh, let us make this our slogan for Christ! The unsaved world is entitled to *know* that Jesus is coming. We are recreant to the trust Christ places in us as believers, as members of his body, as his ambassadors, if we do not deliver this message. Jesus is coming! Are you ready for him? That is the searching question he would have us ask souls everywhere.

The little book bearing that title, "Jesus is Coming," by W. E. Blackstone,[1] is one of the blessedest books to read, and to study, and to give others to read, on this central truth. God has blessed its message during the last twenty or thirty years, having it translated into many different languages, and sending it throughout the world to lead unnumbered thousands into the joy of looking for their Lord.

The Business Men's War Council of the Pocket Testament League (J. Lewis Twaddell,

[1] Published by Fleming H Revell Co., 158 Fifth Avenue, New York City, paper, 30 cents; cloth, 60 cents.

Treasurer, 520 Witherspoon Building, Philadelphia) recently received a letter from a Y. M. C. A. secretary in one of the southern camps, asking them to tell him of some book that would give him the facts about Christ's second coming. For, said he, the soldiers were asking him to tell them about this, and he wanted to be able to do so.

A gray-haired police officer in Philadelphia recently, as my wife made room in a crowded trolley car so that he could get a seat, thanked her, and then fell into conversation with her; and in a moment or two he let fall a remark that disclosed that he was looking for the return of Christ. He was evidently a devout Christian, and he knew the Word of God. He saw no solution for the way in which the age is going save the personal return of Jesus himself.

There is probably more literature on the subject of our Lord's return today than in any time since his ascension. What does this mean? Is it an accident? Or is God himself bringing it to pass that, as the end of the age draws near, the truth of Christ's coming shall be rescued from the well-nigh oblivion into which it had fallen, and people be given a fair opportunity to know this part of the Gospel which belongs to them because "God so loved the world"?

If one has honest doubt as to what the truth concerning our Lord's return really is, let him try the plan a friend of mine followed when he wanted to silence some people who were going after him in this matter.

He was a Princeton football player in his undergraduate days; and he went out to India as a missionary, big in body, mind and heart. He had been trained, as so many good Christian people are, to suppose that the world is getting better, and that the churches are going to Christianize the world, and that at some vague, far distant day when the world has gotten to be a miniature heaven through the influence and power of the Church on earth, Christ will come back again.

In his mission station in India there were some women missionaries from Great Britain who were eager believers in the blessed hope of our Lord's return. When they found that he was not, they started in to set him right! They did this very persistently, quoting Scripture to him with great freedom. He stood his ground against them, but he found himself unable to give them as direct Scripture to prove his position as they were to prove theirs.

So he decided to meet them on their own ground, and to silence them. He went at it in a systematic, honest way. He took his Bible, and a notebook, and he started in to study the Word of God in order to bring together the passages that should show that he was right and they were wrong. Every passage that seemed to prove his position he set down under a certain classification; if there were any passages that seemed to be in favor of their position, he set them under another classification. And so he went faithfully on with his Bible study for several months. At the end of that time, he told me, he was ready for them. "But," he said, "the only trouble was that when I had got my material all together I discovered that they were right and I was wrong. There was no other conclusion to reach from the Bible itself!"

You will not find many persons who have honestly sought out what God says about Christ's coming, who come to any other conclusion. It is human reason, human opinions, our natural, not God's supernatural, views, that deny the coming of Christ to this earth to do here what he has never asked his Church even to attempt to do: establish righteousness on the earth and Christianize society and the world.

How shall we bring the blessed hope into our evangelistic message?

Make the ringing declaration, quietly but earnestly and with a conviction that men cannot escape, that *Jesus is coming*. We shall have explained, if we are following any such simple plan as this little book outlines, why men are lost, and how men are saved. We shall have told about Jesus, and why he had to die if men were to be saved; we shall have told that his death paid the penalty of all who have sinned, and that all he asks us to do is to believe on him and be saved.

Then, is the time to bring out the blessed truth that Jesus is coming again—and are you ready to have him come? If he should come today, would you be glad?

"Nothing is as certain as death and taxes," people say cynically. It doesn't happen to be true. Taxes may be reasonably certain in this life; but death is by no means certain for the Christian. An entire generation of Christians, with all the millions that this may mean, are never going to have the experience of physical death. Tell people this; it will startle many of them. You may never die! If you have taken Jesus as your Saviour, or if you will take him as your Saviour now, and if he comes in your lifetime, as he may, you will never know physical death. "We shall *not* all sleep," rang out Paul's infallible, Spirit-given message, speaking as a believer to believers of the Christian era, "but we *shall* all be changed." Not every Christian will die; but all Christians, both the dead and the living, will be changed at the coming of Christ as they receive their glorious, incorruptible resurrection bodies. For "we which are alive and remain unto the coming of the Lord . . . shall be caught up together with them [the believing dead who are then raised from the dead] in the clouds, to meet the Lord in the air: and so shall we ever be with the Lord" (I Thess. 4:15, 17).

Let us tell men how plainly the Bible, from Genesis to Revelation, records with inspired accuracy the course of the various historical dispensations, or ages of mankind on this earth; how every such age has begun by God's giving men opportunity to believe on him and serve him and be blessed; how the majority of men's response, without exception through the ages, has been to reject the opportunity God has thus repeatedly given them, with the result that mankind has gone down-grade in each age, sinking so low that God in his mercy had to end the age with judgment and punishment for man's sin, and then has given mankind another opportunity and a fresh start.

John Kelman, of Edinburgh, tells of having been in America some years ago and having an interesting discussion with a leading American layman about this great country and its possibilities. Kelman asked the American what, as he saw it, was America's greatest need. Promptly came the reply, "America's greatest need is a king, an absolute monarch."

"What!" exclaimed the Scotchman. "A king in this great democracy! What do you mean by that?"

The Blessed Hope

"Yes," came the quiet reply; "and we know the man. His name is Jesus Christ."

Not until the King comes, in personal, visible presence to establish his kingdom on earth, bringing all lands and all men under his personal reign, will America's problem be solved, or the problems of any nation on earth. But this is not a vain hope; this is our Blessed Hope; for the King is coming.

God is honoring the teaching of Christ's coming, as never before, perhaps, in the Christian era; because Christ's coming is nearer than it ever was before. And what more fitting than that God should see to it that the doctrine of our Lord's return should be given unmistakable proclamation just before the King comes!

It is not a visionary or speculative doctrine. God's Word is never speculative. God's Word is the Rock of Ages; other things are uncertain indeed, but with God there "is no variableness, neither shadow of turning" (James 1:17); "one jot or one tittle shall in no wise pass from the law, till all be fulfilled" (Matt. 5:18).

The truth of our Lord's return is one of the most *practical* truths in human life. It affects daily life; it can and it ought to dominate daily life. God means that it should. It is not *a* doctrine of the Bible; it is *the* doctrine of the Bible. From the time when, through some mystery, Satan was permitted of God to become the

63

"prince of this world" (John 14: 30), things have not been as they should be, and things can never be as they should be, until the rightful Prince of this world comes back, casts out the usurper, and takes his own place on the throne that belongs to him.

Dr. A. C. Dixon, the great Bible teacher and evangelist, now pastor of Spurgeon's famous church in London, tells of an incident in his own family life. He went away from home on a trip, having told his wife that he did not know just when he could return, but that he would come back at the earliest possible moment.

The next morning his little girls said to their mother, "Mother, may we put on our white dresses today, so that we can go down to the train to meet father if he should come back?" They were allowed to do this, and were on the lookout for their father; but he did not come.

The next day they made the same request, and again they were allowed to wear their white dresses; and their mother noticed that they were scrupulously careful all day long not to let any spots get on them.

This went on, day after day, through the week; and the children had never before kept themselves so fresh and sweet and clean. When finally the time came that their father did return, he found his children expectantly awaiting him, dressed in their clean white dresses, and rejoicing to see him, because they were ready and prepared.

✳ We shall keep clean if we are looking for Jesus' return. God asks us to do so. "Every man," he says, "that hath this hope in him purifieth himself, even as he [Christ] is pure" (I John 3:3). The inspired writer has just been speaking of our Lord's coming; a few verses earlier (2:28) he pleads with his Christian readers to "abide in him; that, when he shall appear, we may have confidence, and not be ashamed before him at his coming."

No, the Holy Spirit would not bring a doctrine into mention more than three hundred times in the New Testament, on an average of once every twenty verses, if it were not a vital and a practical doctrine.

Howard A. Banks, Associate Editor of The Sunday School Times, who for four years was Private Secretary to Mr. Daniels, Secretary of the United States Navy, says that when, after years of Christian life, he himself came to see the truth of our Lord's return, it came into his life like a second conversion.

A friend in Mr. Banks' boyhood home had been led to attend the church of Dr. James H. Brookes, in St. Louis. Dr. Brookes was one of the faithful teachers of the truth of our Lord's return. This business man heard that truth preached there, and he became so interested in it that he had a personal interview with the minister.

As a business man he had been in the habit of taking a glass of beer every day after his mid-day lunch, though he had never been an intemperate drinker. The day after his personal talk with Dr. Brookes he went into a saloon and ordered his usual glass of beer. As he lifted the glass to his lips the thought came into his mind, "What if the Lord should return at this moment?" Quickly he set the glass down on the bar, handed the bartender the price of the drink, turned on his heel and left that saloon. He had not touched a drop in that glass, and he did not touch another drop during the rest of his life. Never again did he enter a saloon except to hunt for lost sheep and lead them to Jesus,—for he became a marvelous soul-winner. "I rarely knew," says Mr. Banks, "of any Christian doctrine to transform a man's life as completely as the hope of the Lord's coming transformed this friend of my boyhood days."

Other practical results that the Blessed Hope will have in the believer's life have been brought together by some one in the following list. The truth of the Lord's return makes one:

1. Sober (Luke 12:45; I Thess. 5:1-7).
2. Patient (Jas. 5:7, 8).
3. Moderate ("gentleness") (Phil. 4:5).

4. Charitable (not judging others) (I Cor. 4:5).
5. Diligent (Luke 12:42, 43).
6. Pure (I John 3:2, 3).
7. Always abiding in Christ (I John 2:28).

Christ's coming has been the earth's greatest need since sin entered the universe and the human race; it is the world's greatest need today. And God does not let the world's greatest need go unmet. Christ is coming again.

A Japanese Christian whose ministry has been greatly blessed of God, Kanzo Uchimura, says that there have been three great moments in his life:

"A great moment in my life was when I found myself—or rather, was found by God—to be a sinner. For years my supreme effort was to make myself pure and holy before him.

"Another great moment was when I found my righteousness, not in me, but in him who was crucified for my sins. For years I have tried to realize in myself and others the gospel of Jesus Christ and him crucified.

"A third, and perhaps the last great moment of my life, was when I was shown that my salvation is not yet, and that when Christ shall appear again, then, and not till then, shall I be like him.

"Conviction of sin, salvation by faith, and hope of his coming,—these are three steps by which my soul was lifted to the joy and freedom of the heavenly vision."

VI

SALVATION FROM SIN NOW

The Victorious Life

A MAN had a friend who stammered, and he was enthusiastically telling his friend about a certain institution where stammering could be cured. "You really must go and t-t-try it," he said; "it c-c-c-cured me."

As witnesses for Christ, telling others about the power of Christ over sin, we don't want to be in the position of that man who was "c-c-c-cured." But is it not true that a good many Christians *are* in that position? Can Christ deliver from the power as well as from the penalty of sin? He says he can. Do we believe him? We say we do. But are we delivered? What is the matter?

Fellow Christians, we *must* get the truth about the Victorious Life. It is the key to everything. It means power for service. It means peace—there is no peace without victory. It means joy—perpetual joy, undefeatable joy. It means a testimony that neither man nor Satan can deny.

Set it down, first of all, that the Victorious
Life is the effortless life; effortless so far as
victory is concerned. We do not get victory over
sin by our efforts. For it is a life in which we
are made free; and the man who is made free
does not have to use his efforts either to get himself free or to keep himself free—it is done for
him. Having told the Jews the unwelcome truth
that they were in bondage to sin, our Lord
showed them the way out when he said, "If the
Son therefore shall make you free, ye shall be
free indeed" (John 8:36). Paul knew the
secret, as he exulted in the fact that "the law of
the Spirit of life in Christ Jesus hath made me
free from the law of sin" (Rom. 8:2). We do
not win our freedom. It has been won for us.

That is the meaning of grace: something that
God does for us, not something that we do for
ourselves.

And our salvation is all of grace. Each of
the three parts of our threefold salvation is of
God's grace.

The third and last part of our salvation, which
is our glorification, will be brought to pass when
Christ comes again, as we shall be caught up to
meet him in our resurrection bodies. We are
not told that we shall have to spring up to meet
him! No; it is going to be done for us; without
any effort of our own we shall be caught up,
and so shall we ever be with the Lord (I Thess.
4:17).

The Victorious Life

The first part of our threefold salvation, which is our justification, has been done for us. "You did he make alive, who were dead in trespasses and sins" (Eph. 2:1). You did not make yourself alive; it was done for you, by the grace of God in Christ Jesus. "For by grace are ye saved through faith; and that not of yourselves: it is the gift of God" (Eph. 2:8). The dead man is saved by what God does for him, not by what he does for God—for he can do nothing. Remember, grace never means a joint effort; it does not mean co-operation between God and man to accomplish man's salvation. God is a jealous God; he must do it all, or it will not be done at all. For he knows that that is our only hope. Grace shuts out our worthless, impotent works, and works for us in triumphant omnipotence.

If the first and the third parts of our threefold salvation are wholly of God's grace, being accomplished for us, not by us, so also is the second part, or our sanctification. Sanctification is only another way of saying the Victorious Life. Every Christian recognizes that he is justified by faith and faith alone, and that when he is glorified it will be only because of his faith in Christ, being done wholly for him; yet most Christians do not realize that they can have present victory over sin only on the same terms: that they let God do it all for them, and do not try to help him or share with him in the work.

71

"For if, when we were enemies, we were reconciled to God by the death of his Son, much more, being reconciled, we shall be saved by his life" (Rom. 5:10) ; as Bishop Moule has rendered this, "We shall be kept safe in his life."

But what is the difference between victory over sin in this way, and the victory that is the usual experience of the Christian? The usual experience of the Christian is that he gets victory *by trying for it, instead of by trusting for it.* And it is a counterfeit victory.

The story told of the apparently sweet-spirited old Quaker lady, who seemed never to lose her temper, illustrates this. A young girl had been watching her for some time, and finally she came to the old lady and said, in a burst of enthusiasm, "How under the sun do you do it? How is it you always keep sweet? Why, if the things happened to me that I sometimes see happen to you, I couldn't stand it; I should just boil over."

"Well, my dear," answered the old lady, "perhaps I do not boil over, but thee does not know what boiling is going on inside!"

And that incident has often been told as illustrating real Christian victory. It is only a counterfeit. Victory in Christ is not to be "boiling inside" while we successfully conceal from every one how sinful we feel. Victory is being kept from even boiling inside! Victory, in other

72

words, is a miracle. It is not the concealing of something that ought not to be expressed; it is the expressing of that which is within us, or Christ.

An illustration of real victory, not counterfeit, is seen in the life of the young woman missionary in India, who, after many humiliating failures with an uncontrollable temper, finally found that she could trust Christ as completely for her victory as for her salvation. She wrote a letter to a friend about her wonderful new experience in Christ, and as an evidence that something new had happened in her life, she said: "Do you know that for three months now I have not only not once slammed the door in the face of one of these stupid Indian servants who used to get on my nerves so, but I haven't even *wanted* to once in the three months!" That was a miracle. The "boiling inside" had been done away with. She did not have to try not to slam the door; the old desire to do so had gone. She was experiencing the wonder, the joy of effortless victory. The Son had set her free, and she was free indeed.

Suppose you should unexpectedly meet some one who had done you a great injury—had misrepresented you in the most unfair, untruthful way, doing everything possible to injure your reputation. Suppose you had to be with this person for a few minutes, in such circumstances that you could not avoid the meeting, and you must engage in ordinary conversation until the time has passed. And you are a Christian, intending to do the Lord's will and show Christ's spirit in your life at every point. What would be your sensations and experience under such circumstances?

You might breathe a quick prayer for help, stifle down your feelings of resentment, talk courteously with this enemy of yours, refrain from showing any bitterness, keep on talking, and in your heart keep praying for help and asking the Lord to bring the interview to an end as soon as possible; and thus pass through the experience in such a way that a third person watching you would not know what was going on; and then when the incident was over you might praise God for his delivering power and thank him that you had been prevented from saying a single resentful or unkind word.

Or on the other hand, seeing what you were in for in the encounter, you might remember that Christ was your victory, thank him for being responsible for this whole test, without effort praise him for the Holy Spirit's shedding abroad the love of God in your heart at that moment for this enemy, and then go on in quiet, natural conversation, continuing to praise God moment by moment for the wonderful freedom and effortless victory that he was giving you; and, when the minutes had passed and the incident was at an end, feel that you were sorry that it was over, because of the marvelous love and joy and freedom that had flooded your being every moment of the time. You could honestly say to that enemy that you were sorry you had to leave, when the time for leaving came.

The one experience would be a counterfeit victory; the other would be the genuine thing, that victory which only Christ can give, and which he can give only when we cease from our own efforts and let him do it all.

At the end of a day in which all your plans have gone to pieces, all that you had hoped to accomplish has failed of accomplishment, nothing but a succession of unexpected interruptions, some of them seemingly useless, having occurred —are you as filled with joy and thanksgiving at the close of such a day as you were at its start, when you looked forward happily to doing many things that you had been eagerly waiting for an opportunity to do? If your joy is just as great after all your own plans have been "spoiled" through circumstances beyond your control, then you know what victory is, real victory, that victory which is the joy of the Lord, undefeatable and never failing. But the joy that depends upon circumstances is a counterfeit joy, and has no place in the really victorious life.

How are we to have this amazing, miraculous victory over sin, this freedom from the power of sin?

The answer is simple. After we have taken the Lord Jesus as our personal Saviour, we are then to yield wholly to him, and to believe wholly on him. Surrender and Faith are the two secrets, the two conditions, and the only two, of the victorious life of present salvation from sin.

"For Victory—Save: Buy"; thus reads a War Savings poster. And it adds, "Start now."

Use the same letters, and change the words, and we read: "For Victory—Surrender: Believe." And, "Start now!"

Christ must have all there is of us if we are to have him as our victory. "Present your bodies, a living sacrifice, holy, acceptable unto God, which is your reasonable service" (Rom. 12:1). Can we look into the face of our Lord Jesus, by faith, and say in his strength: "Lord Jesus, I am ready to have thy whole will done in my life, now and always, at every point, no matter what it costs"? If we can honestly say this, we have surrendered. We need not be troubled any more as to the surrender part of the matter.

Then, having done our part, the only question that remains is whether Christ will do his part. And, praise God, that is not a question. We do not even need to say that Christ *will* do his part; better than that, he *is* doing his part now. His part is our victory. It is his responsibility to bring us into victory and keep us there. Is he meeting his responsibility? If he is not, he is not Christ. If he is Christ, he always has been, he is at this moment, and he always will through time and eternity, meet his responsibility.

⟶Then we have victory now! For we have Christ; and Christ is our victory. He simply asks us to thank him that his grace *is* sufficient. He pledges us his word that sin shall not have dominion over us, for we are under grace (Rom. 6:14); and his grace is sufficient for us (II Cor. 12:9).

"Faith does nothing; faith lets God do it all." Having yielded ourselves up to the mastery of Christ, having turned ourselves over to him for him to work his whole will in us and through us, our responsibility is ended, so far as victory is concerned. It is God's responsibility; and God is faithful; God is able (I Cor. 1:9; II Cor. 9:8).

God's faithfulness to me, through Jesus Christ my Saviour, is my victory. That is all I need to know. That is my Rock of Ages. All eternity will not be long enough to finish thanking him for this.

BOOKS AND PAMPHLETS FOR
EVANGELISTIC WORKERS

Scofield Reference Bible.
(Oxford University Press, New York City. $2.00 to $14.00.)

Christian Workers' Testament.
With introduction and compact guide for the use of Scripture in personal soul-winning, by J. Wilbur Chapman and Ralph C. Norton. (The Sunday School Times Company, Philadelphia. Cloth, 75 cents; leather, $1.50; pigskin, $2.00.)

Gospel of John, Underscored Edition.
(Bible House of Los Angeles, Los Angeles, Cal. 33 cents a dozen; $2.45 a hundred copies; cloth, 45 cents a dozen; $3.45 a hundred.)

Rightly Dividing the Word of Truth.
By C. I. Scofield, D.D. (Loizeaux Bros., New York City. 35 cents, cloth; 15 cents, paper.)

Salvation.
By Lewis Sperry Chafer. (Philadelphia School of the Bible, Philadelphia. 75 cents.)

Satan.
By Lewis Sperry Chafer. (Christian and Missionary Alliance Publishing Company, 692 Eighth Avenue, New York City. 60 cents.)

Shall Hell Be Vacated?
By Jesse Forrest Silver. (Bible Institute Colportage Association, Chicago. 15 cents net.)

Without Excuse.
By Arthur J. Smith, D.D. (Glad Tidings Publishing Company, Lakeside Building, Chicago. 10 cents each; three for 25 cents; fifteen for $1; in leather, 25 cents each.)

Taking Men Alive.
By C. G. Trumbull. (Association Press, New York. 60 cents, cloth; 40 cents, paper.)

The Art of Soul-Winning.
By J. W. Mahood. (Abingdon Press, New York. 25 cents net.)

Answered or Unanswered.

By Miss Louisa Vaughan (Missionary Press Co., 1145 North Topeka Avenue, Wichita, Kan. 85 cents, postpaid.)

How to Speak Without Notes.

By Robert E. Speer. (The Sunday School Times Company, Philadelphia. 20 cents.)

"Do" or "Done."

By Charles H. Macintosh. (J. T. Dean, 2613 Pennsylvania Avenue, Dallas, Tex.)

Twelve Great Facts.

By James H. Brookes, D D. (St. Louis Tract Depot, 1427 Locust Street, St. Louis, Mo. 14 cents a dozen; 35 cents a hundred, $1.50 for 500 copies; $2.50 a thousand copies.)

Ungodly People, the Only Kind God Saves.

(Bible House of Los Angeles, Los Angeles, Cal. 25 cents a hundred copies.)

A Spiritual Awakening.

By Charles G. Finney. (Association Press, New York. 5 cents.)

"Suppose"

(Great Commission Prayer League, 808 North La Salle Street, Chicago. Sent free of charge.)

Studying the Second Coming for Yourself.

By James M. Gray, D.D. (Bible Institute Colportage Association, Chicago. 5 cents each.)

Is the Truth of the Lord's Return a Practical Matter for Today?

By C. G. Trumbull. (The Sunday School Times Company, Philadelphia. 4 cents each; 40 cents a dozen, postpaid.)

Why Are We to Believe the Bible Is Inspired?

By I. M. Haldeman, D.D. Challenging fearlessly the denial of inspiration so alarmingly prevalent today. (The Sunday School Times Company. 2 cents each; 20 cents a dozen; fifty or more at 1 cent each.)

What Is It to Believe on Jesus?

By I. M. Haldeman, D D. Eloquent with the dynamic of God, comes a message on God's extraordinary method of redemption for lost men. (The Sunday School Times Company. 2 cents each; 20 cents a dozen; fifty or more at 1 cent each.)

Conversations With a Christian Scientist.

By Judson B. Palmer, General Secretary Emeritus of the Galveston Y. M. C. A. A true story of a Christian Scientist's miraculous conversion. (The Sunday School Times Company. 2 cents each; 20 cents a dozen, or $1.50 a hundred.)

The Life That Wins.

By Charles Gallaudet Trumbull. This little personal message is now having its opportunity to tell in seven different languages of the infinite sufficiency of the Lord Jesus. The author's own edition of the pamphlet, revised and somewhat fuller than in its earlier forms. (The Sunday School Times Company. 2 cents each; 20 cents a dozen; $1.50 a hundred.)

Real and Counterfeit Victory.

By Charles Gallaudet Trumbull. A plain, easily grasped statement of the vast difference between real and counterfeit victory, and the Scriptural basis of real victory over the power of sin. (The Sunday School Times Company. 3 cents each; 30 cents a dozen; $2 a hundred.)

Victory's Final Secret.

A message for baffled ones, and for all who would know and take the final step for victory that is satisfying and Scriptural. Printed in exceptionally beautiful form. (The Sunday School Times Company. 20 cents a dozen, or 75 cents for fifty.)

For Other Literature—

Admirable leaflets for soul-winning work may be had, in large varieties, from:

Bible Institute Colportage Association, 826 North La Salle Street, Chicago.

Bible House of Los Angeles, 643 South Olive Street, Los Angeles, Cal

Asher Publishing Company, 261 Minnesota Street, St. Paul, Minn.

Fred Kelker, Box 216, Harrisburg, Pa.

Bible Truth Depot, Swengel, Pa.

Christian Life Literature Fund, 600 Perry Building, Philadelphia.

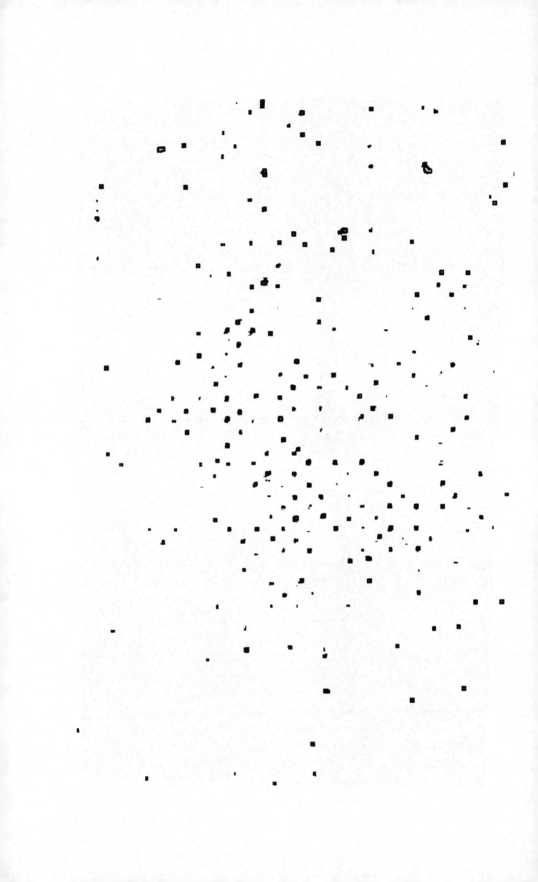

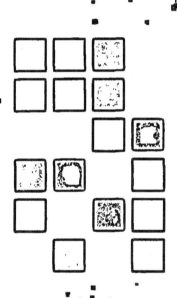

CPSIA information can be obtained
at www.ICGtesting.com
Printed in the USA
LVOW13s1109230117

521859LV00010B/163/P